Seeing the World

BY DICK DAVIS

POETRY
In the Distance   1975
Seeing the World   1980
The Covenant   1984

TRANSLATION
Attar: The Conference of the Birds   1984
(with Afkham Darbandi)

CRITICISM
Wisdom and Wilderness: The Achievement
   of Yvor Winters   1983

EDITION
Thomas Traherne: Selected Writings   1980

Dick Davis
Seeing the World

Anvil Press Poetry

First published in 1980
by Anvil Press Poetry Ltd
69 King George Street London SE10 8PX
Reprinted in 1984
ISBN 0 85646 061 3

This book is published
with financial assistance from
The Arts Council of Great Britain

Set in Monotype Baskerville
Printed in England at
The Arc & Throstle Press
Todmorden Lancs

To Afkham

Many of these poems have appeared
in *PN Review*; others in *The Critical Quarterly*,
The Southern Review and *Sequoia*. 'Climbing'
appeared as a card published by The
Mandeville Press. Grateful acknowledgement
is made to their editors.

Contents

Travelling

1 *Pastoral*

Wild lavender and mint;
                        the mind's bemused
Sheep browse – cropping the serious anecdote,
Eschewing the dust of small-talk.
                                    Nearby,

Reason is a small boy who throws stones, sends
His yapping dog, to guide the errant flock.

2 *An Arrival*

Stranger, accept the little that is given –
The evening crowds, the quick unlooked-for smile
And the benediction of the sunset:
                                    who knows
But the tryst with the unknown god is here?

Desert Stop at Noon

The house is one bare room
And only tea is served.
The old man, mild, reserved,
Shuffles into a gloom
Where mattresses are laid.
I sip, grateful for the cool shade.

His small son watches me,
Approaches, pertly smiles.
I know that thirty miles
Without a house or tree
Surround their crumbling shack.
I drink again, relax, smile back.

Water? and the boy's mother?
Both seem impossible –
Yet, here, my glass is full;
If I ask for another
The boy brings bitter tea
Then grins gap-toothed and begs from me.

And love? Impertinence
To ask. I could not grieve,
Born here, to have to leave:
But he, a man, years hence,
His life elsewhere, may weep
With need to see his father sleep

Again, as now he does,
In careless honesty –
Too old for courtesy –
Oblivious of us.
I pay, and leave the shade,
The dark recess these lives have made.

Night on the Long-Distance Coach

At last it is too dark to read.
I stare out on indifference,
A moonlit world that does not need
Our charity or deference.

And there my unfleshed face stares back,
Thin ghost through which far mountains show,
A palimpsest whose features lack
The constancy that lies below.

Below lie rock and scrub, the plain
Whence rodent eyes peer into mine –
An instant of inhuman pain
Deranges all I would define –

And I, and those I journey to,
Seem shadows without consequence,
A ghostly bustling to and fro
Through wastes of lunar permanence.

The City of Orange Trees

'The city filled with orange trees
Is lost', which, interpreted, meant
All conspicuous luxuries
Augur ruinous punishment.

This fitted what he knew. The zeal
For conquest, prayer, decays; the child
Mocks pieties he cannot feel
And children's children are beguiled

By comfort, gardens, literature.
Aesthetics dazes them, safe lives
Grow lax and soon they can endure
No one but slaves, musicians, wives . . .

Till to degeneracy the Lord
Sends one who, like their forbears, spurns
Mere taste as mannered cant. The sword
Falls and the plundered city burns.

*　*　*

Heir to three generations' learning,
He closed his book, his masterpiece.
Silk rustled as he rose, turning,
Ready to parley now for peace

With one beyond the city gate
Who, barbarous, impatient, vain,
No vows or presents could placate –
The world-conqueror, Tamburlaine.

Syncretic and Sectarian

If, unbeguiled by that suspicious wraith
Called Purity, we look with favour on
   The nebulous, syncretic faith
Of Shah Jahan's first-born, unworldly son –

(Translating Hindu scriptures into Persian,
Convinced the saddhu and the sufi were
   Lost brothers squabbling for the version
Of one tremendous truth) we must refer,

As well, to that blunt, younger brother who
– Contemptuous of vapid heresy –
   Was more than eager to pursue
(By fratricide) the wraith of Purity.

Memories of Cochin

an epithalamium

Through high defiles of warehouses that dwarf
With undetermined age the passer-by,
    We walk toward the ancient wharf,
Assailed by smells – sweet, pungent, bitter, dry:

The perfumed plunder of a continent.
To this shore Roman, Moslem, Christian, Jew
    Were gathered by the dense, sharp scent;
Absorbed now in the once-outlandish view

They camped by hills their children would call home.
So in the soil blurred Roman coins are found;
    Saint Thomas stepped into the foam
And strode ashore, and blessed the acrid ground;

Jews settled here when Sion was laid waste,
And Arabs edged tall dhows into the bay,
    Dutch burghers felt their northern haste,
Becalmed by slow siestas, ebb away . . .

So many faiths and peoples mingle here,
Breathing an air benign with spice and scent,
    That we, though strangers, should not fear
To invoke, in honour of our sacrament,

The sensual, wise genius of this place.
Approach, kind god: bestow your gifts on two,
    Your votaries, of different race
Made one, by love, by marriage, and by you.

Me, You

I am deceived
At first, but no –
You are asleep.
As if you grieved
For some lost glow
Of love, your deep

Dream moves your hand
To seek my skin
And there discover
The well-known land:
Somewhere within
Your brain a lover

Leaves you and you
Reach out to hold
Him close. I touch
Your body too –
As if he told
You what you clutch

Toward, your sleep
Grows still – and now
My hand explores
The silent deep
Of breast and brow.
My hand withdraws.

Now sleep is ours,
Quiet, till dawn
Will wake us to
The separate hours
And we are torn
Apart – me, you.

Marriage as a Problem of Universals

for Meera and Navin Govil

Marriage is where
The large abstractions we profess
Are put gently in their small place –
The holist's stare
In love with Man has managed less
Than eyes that love one ageing face.

Marriage believes
The universals we desire
Are children of a worldly care –
While Plato grieves
For stasis, the refining fire
Men pass through is the lives they share.

Marriages move
Between the symbol and life's facts,
From Beauty to this troubled face –
Though what we love
Is Truth, Truth flares and fades in acts
Of local, unrecorded grace.

The Romantic

Who courts hyperbole
Prefiguring the cost,
Conjures from vacancy
The shores where he is lost –

(The dromomaniac knows
No vale is paradise;
Sad Juan regrets the rose
He knew would not suffice) –

To win must be to lose
And to arrive, depart:
He cannot choose but choose
What lacerates the heart.

Don Giovanni

The unkissed mouth, unsubjugated eyes
Flower in the vacant air . . .

slashed down they rise

In mocking, gossipy, distracting swarms,
A ghastly hydra of unconquered forms . . .

He rides forward. Poor knight, poor travesty –
His quest uncertain, his adversary
At once monotonous and protean,
His loneliness immense, his armour gone
Except the shield,

which bears this sad device
'I know that something somewhere will suffice'.

'Vague, vagrant lives...'

Vague, vagrant lives, elusive, almost,
As the vision that they seek, at home
Nowhere . . .
        they pause before each landscape
With impartial eyes, as if they stood
Here only to collate, compare, then
Move again, assured . . .
            drawn still nearer
To an understanding not yet found.

Government in Exile

Silence, and on the wall the photographs –
Farms, mountains, faces; the sad specifics
Corrode the heart, sharpen the will. Despair
Is shrugged away and stares one in the face.

Loyalty is poured out – a libation
To childhood villages, to stones, to trees.

Metaphor

Emotion flares, and is absorbed: almost
At peace you watch the opalescent west.
Light fades: a flock of birds starts up and wheels
And scatters in the sky, and recombines,
And settles as the first stars shine, intense
As loss, small points of agony, sharp signs
That glitter in the sky's immense grey waste.

Climbing

Enter the clarity you love –
The high thin air above the clouds
That in the wintry wind disperse
Like a mind clearing, like the fading
Of a loved illusion
                    so that you see
The world with unencumbered eyes.

Here, at the summit, at your feet,
Stretches the black volcanic pool,
The dark Avernus of the self.

Dawn

You cannot say what sense it is through which
You understand but it is like the wind
That gently chill-ly tugs the desert plants
And leaves them undisturbed or like the air
That preternaturally reveals the hills
Or like the silence through which nothing sounds
Like words. Light spreads and speaks. You understand
It is that truth you need not understand.

Dying

Illness, and prayer.
From the window
Darkness: his stare
On the dark snow.

The nurse: in her
Hands reality,
A glinting blur –
A certainty.

Prayer and dark snow.
The nurse recedes.
She is real, though
Not what he needs.

The Messenger

Years now since you have stood
Insistent at my door
Speaking with silent eyes
Of that still-silent shore –

Years now since I have risen
Resistless at your call
And stretched my hand in greeting
As if there loomed no wall

Between the dead and living –
As if I too might go
Where darkness would redress
Intolerable woe.

And now that with this dusk
You have returned, I rise
To read once more the silence
Of dark, remembered eyes.

Zuleikha Speaks

Gentle, then cruel – the same
Half-masked indifference
Dulls both. I say your name,
'Husband'. With what loathed sense

Am I yours, you mine? Night
Gives me to you but I
Shrink from its shameful rite,
Your energy and sigh,

The weight you think I love:
And in the day you watch,
Laugh, grumble, bargain – move
Beyond my woman's touch.

Now though you are not here.
I see the goats brought in,
The gilded dust, and hear
The world's unfocused din –

(Kids' startled hooves, boys' cries,
Somewhere a flute). The dim
Gold twilight weakens, dies.
I stay. I think of him,

The stranger –
        as reticent,
Ineffable, as is
This sun's unprized descent.
I know that I am his.

The cold wind stirs my dress.
The desert stars appear.
My husband calls. I bless
His name, but shall not hear.

Simeon

Luke II.26

How long now since
The vow was made . . .
Yet still he haunts
The temple's shade

Silent to those
Who say he dreamed
The angelic face.
Its splendour gleamed

More harshly than
The sacral knife
Caught by the sun,
And seared his life

To a blank daze
Of memory . . .
The half-glimpsed face
Of certainty.

As if that pause
When Abraham
Through lawless tears
Beheld the ram

Had been delayed
For centuries,
The falling blade
As on a frieze.

St Christopher

Curled fingers tighten in his curly hair:
But if, by any prescience, he knows
The nature of that burden He must bear
Whom now he bears, no recognition shows.

The weathered body and tenacious mind
Venture like partners with but one intent –
Lo, they are one, as cautiously they find
The safe stones through the unsafe element.

And thus, subsumed by what he does, made sure
That though his task is humble it is good,
He navigates toward the further shore –
Secure in skill and patient hardihood.

Winter

Your moment comes, inapprehensible.
Autumnal cold pervades the mountain pool;
The tense, still surface glistens; it is ice.
I peer, but cannot see what lives or dies.

Quotidian despair, I feel your cold lips
Searching me in the dark, your soft hand grips
With an enormous strength: I tremble, yours.
It is your hand that guides me now, explores

The vacant world for me.
                                    I walk at night,
Possessed by the cold: on a building-site
Smoke from the watchman's fire smarts in my eyes:
Brief greetings clash, like gravel thrown on ice.

Withernsea

Stones, sand, I have not seen in fourteen years;
A place for childhood's self-communing tears,

For wandering. I walked the moonlit beach
An adolescent whom no waves could teach

The simplest truth of life, that nothing lasts:
I scavenged among poetries and pasts

For something glittering, precise and sure.
In winter-storms gigantic breakers tore

The cliff's vermilion mud into the sea.
The weakening edge seeps vaguely, constantly.

Baroque Opera

House-lights go down, the velvet curtains rise –
Sea-fights, magicians and Cortona skies,

Grand rage. But soon the god from a machine
Back stage will rearrange the wrecked, sad scene

And each persona hear his proper due –
The reach of evil blocked, the righteous few

(Young, wise, made safe by love) presented their
Just prize – salvation from despair and care.

They are our golden representatives
And share the exigence of makeshift lives –

The rope let down into contingent fact,
The hope never defined and always lacked.

A Recording of Giuseppe de Luca
(1903)

The record's hiss – so dense
You hardly hope to hear
The voice rise sweet and clear
Beyond its violence –

Seems like the sea-wash of
Time's old opacity
As it indifferently
Obscures the things we love.

But with what poignant strength
The voice soars free of time –
The young man in his prime
Still careless of the length

Of laggard years ahead,
Of that attrition which
No beauty can bewitch . . .
The youth so long now dead.

False Light

See where the landscape glows and flares
Lit by the beacons of desire –

As faces grouped about a fire
Give back the light that is not theirs.

Opening the Pyramid

Though you recall the emphatic starlight
When the angels said, 'Follow, we shall lead',

Irony, like the free air and sunlight,
Crumbles the mummy of each simple creed.

Wittgenstein in Galway

O come unto these yellow sands
Alone.
       The slow work of his hands,

Secluded by sad policy,
His hut opposed the breaking sea

Whose meaningless unchanged refrain
Might one day still the circling brain.

     *   *   *

Things that could never be thought of
Were metaphysics, anguish, love.

And though his tamed gulls swooped for bread
He lived, like us, inside his head

Locked out of that vast privacy
Of stones and sand, wild gulls and sea.

An Entry

*'When one is frightened of the truth (as I am now) then it is
never the* whole *truth that one has an inkling of.'*
                    – Wittgenstein: *Notebooks*, 15.10.1914

To what strange sum could you be reconciled
That could atone for consciousness adrift
In grandeur it can never comprehend,

For suffering, for death?
                        What glimpse beguiled
You of our fear? What hand disclosed what gift
In token that blind passion has an end?

Philosopher and Metaphysics

If shocked outsiders sympathize
With his neglected, brilliant wife

They have been spared the specious lies,
The skittish charm that wrecked his life.

Two Epigrams on Victory

1

Wotan and Prospero
Grown wise in tribulation know
    Whose is the victory,
And envy his simplicity.

2

Life narrows to the things you did not mean;
The endless vista is a painted screen.

Now, like the Count in *Figaro*, you see
Forgiveness where you ogled victory.

Two Songs

1

Sweet lady do not grieve
That you shall hear no more
His quick licentious wit –
Love's promises deceive
The poorest of the poor
And the purposeless exquisite:

And now that you have lost
One battle in love's war
You seem each opposite
At once – both to your cost –
The poorest of the poor
And the purposeless exquisite.

2

The young girl tilts her head
To his receptive shoulder

And though tonight in bed
New love will seem far colder

Than she had dreamt or read
Feared loneliness will hold her

– Whatever tears are shed –
To his indifferent shoulder.

Love

Later her heart will blur with pain

(He sleeps. Her hand strays in his hair,
Impulsive, indolent.
                              She says,
'I love you' to the morning air.)

Now the years say nothing to her.

A Song of Parting

I had not thought unhappiness
Could pierce again my armoured years –
But I conceived your mute distress
And faltered with your faltering tears.

O who grows old! – not I, though I
Am old to you in wasted years –
My heart was wasted by your sigh,
I faltered with your faltering tears.

Is this then to grow old – to lose
Your dear form to the darkening years?
To know myself, who cannot choose
But falter with your faltering tears?

To Exorcize Regret

Grant the patience to accept
What the heart would still reject

May the distance be mere space
Grant the grace to need no grace

May flesh be flesh –
                              never again
Source and symbol of such pain.

A Perfect Ending

These two now meet
Under no god's tutelage –
  Their smiles, discreet,
Need no reserves of courage:

  These two, who once
Were adepts, are polite –
  These celebrants
Agree to smooth the rite

  To an aesthete's
Memory: renouncing Eros
  Their brisk chat treats
As 'youth' once-frantic loss.

Desire

Of the violence of that pain
What poor traces still remain –

This I learnt: the wry technique
Of avoiding what I seek.

Phaedra and Hippolytus

She felt the virgin's tentative
Thin lips brush stiff against her own –

Reluctant flesh, that would disown
Mere human need, that could not live.

Rembrandt's *Return of the Prodigal Son*

Age instinct with wisdom, love, bends towards
The sensual man, the penitent, and clasps
Him lightly by the shoulder-blades. In rags
The latter kneels and rests his close-cropped head
Against the Father's chest. Some watch, and one,
Whose face is lit, old as the Father, looks
With unobserved compassion at the scene.

His comprehension is the artist's own:
His silence and the Father's flood the frame
But cannot quite subdue the young man's sobs,
The fixed, sad past; the waste that love would heal.

Rembrandt Dying

What have I known?
The darkness I perceived
Beyond each face invades my mind,
I have been shown
The night of the bereaved
In which all men are blind.

But I recall
Old faces marred, their eyes
Outstaring that obscurity –
Awaiting all
Life yet may ask with wise,
Unbroken, dignity;

And the young Jew
Who was my Christ, in whose
As-if-omniscient, worn face
Compassion grew –
Where patience could peruse
The sufferings of a race;

And Hendrickje
Who taught me tenderness,
So that the proof of all technique
Was to convey
Love's truths – light on a dress,
Or on her turning cheek.

All these are past –
    The darkness wells in me;
Though grief and ignorance increase
        And must outlast
    My will, yet memory
    Is thankful for lost peace.

Leonardo

whose Last Supper *began to break up in his own life-time*

My years were given
To permanence –
The arrested dance,
Emblem of heaven.

Decay invades
The icon of
Eternal love:
My emblem fades

Like human skin:
The wrinkles grow
As if paint too
Partook of sin.

Late, late I see
The meaning of
Incarnate love,
Eternity.

On a Painting by Guardi

Slowly the chill lagoon
Returns to flood these noisome ponds;
  Grotesque, dense weeds festoon
The ruined arch with airy fronds

  In whose shade scavengers
– Tenacious as the trailing weeds –
  Time's ghostly avatars,
Indifferent to the grace that feeds

  Their chance cupidity,
Draw strength from glory in decay.
  Great Mutability,
All here declares your mordant sway.

  I gaze, hardly aware
Of this overt, didactic aim:
  Rather the misty air,
The blank, amorphous shore proclaim

  An eye in love with blurred
And insubstantial forms, a mind
  By evanescence stirred –
A suppliant of the undefined,

  The pale marsh-haze of noon;
And one who in each breeze could see
  – Ruffling the chill lagoon –
The tremor of mortality.

Epitaph

I betrayed **and** I was betrayed.
Wistful for righteousness I added to
   The world's evil. Invoke my shade
With gentleness; this grief will be yours too.

Maximilian Kolbe

O crux ave spes unica

Secure, afraid, I contemplate
The fearless necessary fate
Of one who, undisturbed by crime,
Became himself his Paradigm.

Notes

THE CITY OF ORANGE TREES (page 13)
In *An Introduction to History – The Muqaddimah*, Ibn Khaldun quotes and explains the proverb with which this poem opens. The meeting that ends the poem occurred outside the walls of Damascus in 1401.

SYNCRETIC AND SECTARIAN (page 14)
Dara Shukoh, the eldest son of Shah Jahan, translated the *Upanishads* into Persian with the avowed intention of finding common ground between Islam and Hindu beliefs. In 1659 he was murdered by his younger brother, who later became the emperor Aurungzeb, the most fanatically zealous of all the Moghul emperors.

ZULEIKHA SPEAKS (page 28)
Zuleikha is the woman known in the Bible as Potiphar's wife. In one interpretation of the story Zuleikha represents the human soul wedded to the world (Potiphar) but 'illicitly' in love with the beauty of God, represented by Joseph.

WITTGENSTEIN IN GALWAY (page 38)
'(In 1947) . . . he left Cambridge and settled for a while in Ireland . . . in a seaside hut in Galway, where the fishermen remarked on his ability to tame birds.' Anthony Kenny, *Wittgenstein*.

MAXIMILIAN KOLBE (page 55)
In Auschwitz this Polish priest voluntarily took upon himself the death sentence passed on another prisoner.